Guide to Boosting Your Own Self Esteem

Ethan Hale, M. Sc.

www.efhale.com * 405-820-5845 * efhale@efhale.com

Table of Contents

Guide to Boosting Your Own Self Esteem 2
Ethan HaleTable of Contents 2
A Positive Outlook for a Positive Life 4
Know your self-worth 5
The benefits of using positive self-talk 7
How positive affirmations can change your life 9
Chapter II: It's All in Our Mind 11
Focusing the mind on the positive 11
The sky is your limit 13
How to develop your creative side 15
Creativity Tips and Resources 16
Listen to your inner thoughts 18
Mental imagery works 20
Taking care of your mental health 22
Chapter III: Overcoming Negative Thinking 24
Dispelling fears for a more positive outlook 24
Overcoming dissociation 25
Overcoming Doubt 27
Overcoming Feelings of Helplessness 29
Overcoming Inner Conflicts 31
Overcoming Intimidation 32
Overcoming the need to be in control 34
Overcoming Trauma 36
Chapter IV: Becoming an Optimistic Individual and Achieve Goals in Life 38
Developing your self-image 38
Change the Shape of Your Self-Image 39
How keeping a journal can help you succeed 41
Develop your intuition 42
Start Early To Combat Low Self Esteem 43
Stop underestimating your worth 45
Developing your full potential 48
Boost your Self-Esteem by Running 49
How to Unearth Your Hidden Strengths 51
How NLP Can Help You 52
De-cluttering for success 54

www.efhale.com * 405-820-5845 * efhale@efhale.com

unconsciously throughout the day, you can begin to gain more control over every aspect of your life and make essential changes.

Your ability to succeed in life largely depends on how you deal with life, a positive mental attitude leads to a confident and ultimately more successful person than one full of negativity which leads to a lack of self-confidence and low self-esteem. By taking a positive attitude you look at life in a different way to one of negativity, a positive attitude leads to seeing good in people and the world which leads to optimism and success. Your quality of life is based on how you think and feel from moment to moment and changing the way you think can drastically change how you see life and deal with life.

The person who goes through life optimistically with a positive attitude is better able to deal with life and the problems which it sometimes throws at us, they are able to bounce back and recover from problems or set-backs in life. The optimistic person will see the problem for what it is, nothing but a temporary set-back which they can overcome and move on, when looking at life in this optimistic way the person is able to take full control over their thoughts and feelings and turn a negative situation into a more positive one by simply altering the way they think. Since thoughts can either be positive or negative and you can only have one thought in mind at any one time then choosing positive will keep your thoughts, feelings and actions optimistic which leads to a happier person who is able to achieve their goals much easier.

Using positive self-talk in your daily life

You should use positive self-talk throughout the day in order to establish a new thinking pattern, you will probably have established a pattern of negative thinking for many years and this will take time to overcome, to start with you should aim to repeat positive self-talk around 50 times throughout the day, this can be achieved by repeating positive statements quietly to yourself or out aloud. Positive self-talk can be used for many different aspects in your life, it can help you to overcome difficult situations, gain more confidence in yourself, help you to quit habits, recover quicker from illness or make changes to your life in general. Popular phrases or sentences that can be used in positive self-talk include.

- I have an interesting challenge facing me – this could be used when a problem occurs in life or there is some difficulty, rather than looking at the situation in a negative way and thinking I have a problem, thinking of it as a challenge is a much more positive way of dealing with it.
- I like the person I am – this could be used to bolster self-confidence and gain respect about yourself and the person you are, similar statements could be "I am the best", "I am a good person" or "I have many excellent qualities".
- I know I can do this – this could be used if you are faced with a certain task that you would previously doubt yourself capable of conquering, similarly you could say "I have the ability to conquer this" or "this doesn't pose a problem for me"
- I am full of health, energy and vitality – this can be used to encourage good feelings about your health either after you have been sick or while recovering from an illness.
- I am fulfilled as a person – this can be used to encourage good general positive thoughts about yourself and the world in which you live.

How positive affirmations can change your life

Having a positive attitude is the key to being happy and leading a successful life, our thoughts play a huge role in how we feel and positive thinking leads to a confident person happy in life, while negativity leads to low self-esteem and you

www.efhale.com * 405-820-5845 * efhale@efhale.com

missing out on so much in life. We so often talk ourselves out of things without even realising we are doing so, everyday hundreds of negative thoughts drift freely through our mind, we put ourselves down too much and sow the seeds of doubt. There is a small simple tool that you can use throughout the day to help to change these negative thoughts and instil a more positive way of thinking; using daily positive affirmations can change your life drastically for the better. They can make you more confident, more aware, more sure of yourself and change your life in many more aspects for the better.

What are positive affirmations?

Positive affirmations can be used throughout the day anywhere and at anytime you need them, the more you use them the easier positive thoughts will take over negative ones and you will see benefits happening in your life. An affirmation is a simple technique that is used to change negative self-talk that we are rarely even aware of doing, into looking at your life with a more positive attitude. Most of us have for many years bombarded ourselves with negative thoughts so changing your thoughts and the way you think won't happen overnight but if you stick with affirmations they will work once you have retrained your way of thinking. There are many different affirmation techniques for dealing with different situations in life and the most popular and successful are listed below.

The mirror technique

This technique helps you to appreciate yourself and develop self-awareness and self-esteem, you should stand in front of a mirror, preferably a full length one in either just your underwear or better still naked. Start at your head and working down your body say out loud what it is you like about areas of your body, for example you could say "I like the way my hair shines, the slight differences in color where the light hits it" or " my eyes are a lovely shade of _ _ _ _. They sparkle and glint; my eyes are a wonderful feature" take the time and go slowly over all your body building up a more positive image of yourself.

The anywhere technique
This technique can be used anywhere and whenever you catch yourself thinking a negative thought, when you realize you are having a negative thought think of yourself turning down a volume knob inside your head so that you turn it down low enough so as not to hear it any longer. Then think a positive affirmation to replace the negative and turn the volume back up repeating it to yourself.

The trashcan technique
If you have negative thoughts write them down on a scrap of paper, screw the paper up into a ball and throw it into the trashcan, by doing this you are telling yourself these thoughts are nothing but rubbish and that's where they belong.

The meditation technique
Find somewhere quiet where you able to relax for 5 or 10 minutes close your eyes and let your mid empty of all thoughts and feelings. Begin to repeat your affirmation to yourself over and over again while concentrating on the words you are repeating and believe in what you are saying.

Chapter II: It's All in Our Mind

Focusing the mind on the positive

We all go through some tough times in life, that's just life; it can't always be a bed of roses. However life is what you make it and by staying positive through the bad times as well as the good can make all the difference and gets you through the tough times with a smile.

But the big question is "how do you stay positive when things get tough?" Staying upbeat at times like this is the last thing on your mind, but it should be the first, you need to think positively now more than ever. The key to staying positive is to take your mind off your problems and worries and re-energizing your mind, this is especially true when you are having a bad day and you feel sorry for yourself and want to sit down and cry. Here are some excellent tips for keeping a positive outlook in life no matter what's going around you.

- If you find yourself around those who are negative then break free from them, negativity has a way of passing from person to person and they will drag you down with them.
- Don't sit in front of the TV for hours at a time, the news is depressing, cop shops feature violence and death and negativity in some form is found on almost every show. If you do watch TV go for the more positive program such as a nature documentary showing the wonderful world in all its glory or a comedy.
- Spend as much time as you can with your family and loved ones, do something together which you all enjoy and aim to have a family night at least once a week where you can spend quality time together.
- In times when you are feeling particularly low and negativity starts to creep in, listen to a motivational CD or repeat positive affirmations to yourself to bring back a positive attitude.
- Take time out each day to just do something that you enjoy doing that doesn't require you to make choices or decisions, something which relaxes you to the fullest.
- Try doing something that you wouldn't normally do, something that is totally unlike you and out of character, take up a new hobby or sport that you would never have dreamed of doing.
- Get some exercise, this could be something as simply taking a walk in the fresh air and is totally free or go to the gym or taking part in activities such as yoga.

www.efhale.com * 405-820-5845 * efhale@efhale.com

- Set yourself goals in order to get ahead and when you accomplish a goal give yourself a small reward for doing so
- Learn techniques that allow you to bring your attention and focus back to the task on hand quickly.
- Use affirmations throughout the day to instill self-confidence and positive thoughts and feelings.
- Always look for the best in bad situations, while things might not be what we expect if you look hard enough you may find they are not as bad as they seem to be.
- Remember that the situation won't last forever, this is only a temporary stage you are going through and it will get better.

The sky is your limit

You can accomplish anything you set your mind to, the sky really is your limit, and providing you follow a few simple steps, you are able to accomplish anything in life. The key to success is, being absolutely committed to achieving what it is you want, set your mind to taking whatever steps needed to accomplish what you want and you change your approach and stick with this new approach until you achieve what you want. The steps are relatively easy to follow and changes can be made easily to determine your success in anything that you want to achieve in life, let's take a closer look at the above steps.

Commitment
You should take positive action and decide exactly what it is you wish to achieve in life and set your goal, once you have set your mind on what you want you should go into it with utter conviction and commitment. When you are planning and setting out your goal you have to have firm conviction that you will achieve your goal whatever it takes, you should visualize

your goal from beginning to end and see yourself achieving whatever it is you set out do.

Take whatever steps are needed
Once you have decided to go for it and have made the commitment then the next step is to start taking action towards reaching your goal, taking the first step is actually the hardest part because it means going out there and actually doing something. Thinking about what it is you have to do is the easy part as is saying you are committed to doing, but doing means facing the unknown and putting your plan into action and this stage is very often where most people fail, because fear stops us from moving forward.

Sticking with it
When you have made the commitment and taken the plunge into making your dream or goal a reality you have to have perseverance and be willing to change your approach until you finally reach your desired goal. Depending on what it is that you set out to do this could take some time but it essential that you stay as committed to seeing the project through as when you first started out, it can help to keep a journal of your project from start to finish, this way you are able to see how far you have come and keep your mind focused on the outcome you wish to achieve. Life has many unexpected quirks and can throw anything at us so it is important that you continue pushing yourself through any unexpected hard times continually onwards towards your goal. Once again fear is the main problem and the biggest reason why most people fail to achieve and give up what they set out to do, if you give in to fear it will only continue to put bigger blocks in your way until eventually it overcomes you and you give in. The sky really is your limit if you attempt set out to accomplish with perseverance and determination to overcome anything that is thrown into your path.

www.efhale.com * 405-820-5845 * efhale@efhale.com

How to develop your creative side

Everyone has a creative side although sometimes it is hidden and does not come to the surface quite as quickly as it does to others, however you can develop creativity by digging deep and practicing, searching for your creative side and bringing it to the forefront. Here are some top tips for helping you to draw out your creative side and expand on your creativity.

- Create lists – you can expand your creativity greatly and get that side working by making up a list whenever you have a problem which needs some creative thinking, list down as many ideas as you possibly can for solutions and let your creativity flow.
- Make changes in your life – sometimes we can get a creative block if we are stuck in a rut, make some changes to your daily life to get the channels flowing again.
- Work on the bad ideas – even if you are only coming up with bad ideas you are still being creative so work on the bad ones and develop them, whose to say it is a bad idea anyway, it could turn into a great idea and solution to your problems.
- Work in a great – working in a group and brainstorming together is a great way to develop creativity.
- Challenge yourself and others – if you challenge yourself by telling yourself you can't do something the way you always have done it, you will then have to think of new ways to get around the problem which can lead to some very creative suggestions.
- Doodle – if you are stuck for ideas to a solution then keep a pen and paper handy and let your imagination clear and doodle ideas on the paper, it's surprising what you will come up with if you free your mind this way.
- Encourage the thinking side of your brain – the right side of your brain is where the creativity starts so give it

www.efhale.com * 405-820-5845 * efhale@efhale.com

a jolt and wake it up by activating using the left side, try breathing out using only your left nostril a few times.
- Hire a life coach – if you feel your creativity is truly depleted then consider hiring a life coach to help you find it, a life coach can help you to establish the areas where your creativity is lacking and work with you to strengthen it.
- Think like a child – let go of all your adult obligations, stresses, strains and worries and go back to your childhood, children have the best imaginations and their creativity knows no bounds, think like a child when you are stuck for creative ideas and they will soon flow freely once again.
- Relax – creativity can often become depleted if we are under great stress, learning a relaxation technique not only makes you feel better but can help to clear your mind, give you a fresh start and get your creative side flowing again.
- Use some mind games – keep a few mind games to hand such as logic puzzles, by taking your mind off your problem and solving a puzzle you are using your brain and using your brain leads to positive and creative thinking.

Creativity Tips and Resources

Everyone can benefit from creativity in their lives. You can use creativity to help with work projects, goal setting, home and family management and a whole lot more. To help with all of your home and work projects, here are 10 tips to improve your creativity.

1. Stay Healthy
Find an exercise routine that you enjoy and stick to it. Change it when you want to, but keep doing some sort of exercise. Sleep well. Eat a variety of healthy foods. Meditation or

something you like to do to relax can help you keep your mind focused.

2. Explore New Things
We do so many things without thinking about them. These things become our daily routines – the mundane and boring. Try something new. It can be something as little as taking a different route to work or something like taking up a new class in something you have always wanted to learn.

3. Start Thinking Like Curious George
Ask yourself questions about everything you see, hear and read. Why? How? What if? Find out the answers to your questions. You can also keep a curious journal and track all of your findings.

4. Read a New Book
Choose one that you wouldn't normally choose. Pick one up at the library. If you have always preferred reading nonfiction, pick up a fiction book. There are so many interesting books to read and so many different genres to choose from. Your librarian will be happy to help you explore new books.

5. Act Like a Kid
Children are so carefree, honest and fun. Think about what you used to do for fun as a child. Paint a picture, take out those charcoals, get some fingerpaints, go to your local amusement park…anything that a kid would do! And have fun!

6. Everyone Needs a Little "me" Time
Take some time everyday to just relax. You can use meditation if you like to meditate. Don't make any plans, pay any bills…nothing. Just do nothing for a little while.

7. What If?
What is the end of the world was tomorrow? What if you did go to college for business? What if aliens were real? What if there is an afterlife? Make up your own what if questions and just see where your brain takes you.

www.efhale.com * 405-820-5845 * efhale@efhale.com

8. Never Assume Anything
Assuming anything always gets someone in trouble. You might assume that your boss is a jerk. What if he just doesn't like his life and takes it out on his employees? You might assume that the person who cut you off this morning was inconsiderate. What if they were rushing their child to the hospital?

9. Write About You
Who are you? What kind of person are you? Where have you been in your life? When are the most important things in your life? Why do you do things the way you do? How do you live your life each day?

10. Have Conversations with People
Listen closely to what they have to say instead of waiting for your turn to speak. What must it be like to be this person? Imagine how they live and think.

Listen to your inner thoughts

We all have feelings about things that happen in life, they might be discouraging thoughts and feelings or they could be positive ones, an easy example of listening to your inner thoughts is trying on a dress for a special night out. You put the dress on and look in the mirror, you automatically think wow, I look great or shake your head and choose another outfit. This is the simplest form of listening to your inner thoughts or intuition when it comes to making the best decision.

However we can put our inner thoughts to many good uses in our day-to-day living if we open up and tune into them. Our inner thoughts can help us to succeed in life, become more confident and live a happier, more productive and fulfilling life.

You are the most valuable resource that you have in life when it comes to making the right choices and the right decisions. You automatically know if something's right or wrong and how to achieve the best results simply by going along with your own intuition, and it very rarely lets us down.

Channeling into your intuition is easy and here are some simple ways you can start using it:

- Start off the easiest way developing your intuition by using it to make choices for less important decisions, examples could be, choosing what you want for dinner or which movie or restaurant to go to.
- You will find it easier to tune into yourself and your inner thoughts when it is quiet, so choose a room where you know you won't be disturbed when it comes to making important choices and decisions. A good technique to use is to close your eyes and take a couple of deep breaths, focus entirely on the question or task at hand and see what immediately comes to mind.
- Be willing to admit that you might make mistakes when listening to your intuition, while your intuition is usually right, you might misinterpret your inner thoughts that can lead to making a mistake. However you should learn by the mistakes you make and continue developing and strengthening your inner guidance.
- When letting your inner guidance come through don't confuse matters by trying too hard or swaying the answer one way or another, chances are if you are leaning towards going in one direction then you already have the answer.

Following the above is the easiest way to get your inner guidance to start surfacing when you need it, the more you turn to it and use it, the easier it will become. As the cartoon

www.efhale.com   *   405-820-5845   *   efhale@efhale.com

character "Jiminy cricket" sang to his friend Pinocchio "always let you conscience be your guide", the same applies in real life, follow your heart, your inner thoughts and feelings and you will never go far wrong. It is only when we begin to lose faith and doubt ourselves that we become unstuck and indecisive and this leads us in the wrong direction or at a standstill.

Mental imagery works

One of the most powerful and inspirational tools which can be used daily is something which every one of us possesses, our very own imagination. Your own thoughts, insights, ideas and intuition can be used in your daily life to make positive changes for the better in any aspect of your life. Everyone has an imagination although some of us have a more vivid one that springs to life quicker than others do, but with a little practice, we can all form imagery in our mind to benefit us.

Using the imagination as a tool
How you use your imagination to benefit you in your daily life is only limited by you, you can use your imagination to visualize any number of things and use it for almost any situation. Visualization works by forming a positive picture of the outcome of a situation and seeing this positive outcome in your mind as though it's happening and letting it replace any negative thoughts you had. You must develop the visualization as much as you can and look at it from all angles and perspectives, the mental picture which you build in your mind must be as clear as possible of how you wish the situation to turn out. Think of your imagination and the mental picture you build as a blueprint for developing and building on, just as an architect uses a blueprint when designing a project from start to finish.

The foundations
Start by laying out the foundations of your idea or what it is you wish to change in your mind and slowly build up from the bottom, clearly visualizing every little nook and cranny of the idea, the foundation work behind your idea is the basis for your success. When lying down the foundations think about the following

- What is it exactly that I want to achieve or change?
- What difference will this make to make?
- Can I achieve what I want on my own?
- What do I have to change in my life to accomplish this?
- What do I have to learn to accomplish this?

Once you have laid the foundations for whatever it is you wish to change in your life then you can go ahead and build up on your plan, visualize the project every step of the way as clearly as possible and seeing the project from start to finish build in your mind as accurately as possible. When you have the visualization completed in your mind then you can take steps to achieve what it is you desire, if you wish you can then note down the steps you took in your mind in writing to achieve the outcome, and follow these through from start to finish.

The key points
The key points to using mental imagery successfully for any aspect of your life are

- Focusing your imagination on one idea
- Forming as clear a mental picture or image of the idea and outcome in your mind
- Building up the idea from the foundations to completion
- Successfully executing your plan

www.efhale.com * 405-820-5845 * efhale@efhale.com

Taking care of your mental health

In order to live a happier, healthier life you should take care of more than your physical health by way of dieting and exercising, you should also take care of your mental health. Only by having a complete system of healthy living can you be a healthy person, while exercise is important for your body it is also important for your mind.

Stress comes to all of us in some form or other with worries about finances, job security, responsibilities and relationships all taking their toll on our mental health. Stress is one of the biggest factors to disrupting our mental health and ultimately our well-being, it is as important to reduce stress in your life, as it is to reduce your fat, sugar and calorie intake to remain healthy.

There are many ways which we can take care of our mental health and eliminate some of the stress from our day, some of the steps you can take to remain stress free include

- Learn to manage your day and time better by setting out realistic goals which you can manage to meet everyday
- Learn how to utilize your time more efficiently throughout the day by focusing and completing one task at a time before moving on to another
- Remain flexible in your thinking when it comes to completing tasks, if you cannot accomplish them the way you had planned then do it another way
- Take small breaks throughout the day, these will give you time to clear your head and get back on track and stay focused on the task at hand
- Admit that you are only human and you cannot do everything, admit when you need a little help and don't be afraid to ask for that help should you need it'
- Learn when to say "no", while we all like to do favors we can sometimes take too much onto our plates and

www.efhale.com * 405-820-5845 * efhale@efhale.com

when this happens we cannot manage to fit everything in and stress sets in
- Never try to over exert your body, you can only do so much in a day, by trying to push yourself continually beyond your limits will stress your body and mind
- Learn to recognize when you are starting to get stressed and take immediate action to relieve that stress
- Learn techniques which you can quickly eliminate stress, there are a wide range of techniques which you can use, with some working better than others and giving you better results. Techniques such as breathing exercises and visualization are very effective measure which can be used to quickly ease stress and let you refocus
- Positive affirmations can help you deal with stress effectively, a positive mind with positive thoughts is a healthier mind and one to stress less eagerly
- Always make time for some quiet time, time to just relax and do something you enjoy and don't feel guilty for taking this time out

Chapter III: Overcoming Negative Thinking

Dispelling fears for a more positive outlook

Fears and phobias are something which can have an affect on anyone to some extent, while most of us can conquer our fear and most fears and phobias are dislikes more than actual phobias, for some people fear and phobia can be severely distressing and have a huge impact on their day-to-day living.

Fear and phobias obviously cause negativity and constant negativity gets us down, while some phobias and fear can be deep-seeded you can break the hold it has over you with time and help. There are various methods of help, and the more deeply seeded the fear or phobia, the more likely professional help may be advised in the form of a therapy or hypnotherapy. If the fear is only mild then you may overcome it by using self-help methods.

Understanding fears and phobias
In order to be able to conquer fears and phobias it is essential that you understand them, fear and phobia simply causes us uncomfortable thoughts and feelings when placed in certain situations. It can bring feelings such as nausea, vomiting, dizziness, a terrible feeling, a tight band of pressure around the head, pains in the chest, a feeling of breathlessness and trembling. These are all feelings that we ourselves allow to build up and take over our mind and body, dispelling fear is a matter of taking back control and putting things into perspective.

This is the basis behind curing any form of fear or phobia although if you suffered for many years it will take longer for you to recover, recovery is possible. Phobias and fear are basically exaggerated anxiety, and learning methods and ways to relax is a good start to curing fear and phobias. There are many self-help books, DVDS, courses and audio courses that can help you make a start, any self-help material designed for dealing with anxiety and stress will help but there are many specifically aimed at those suffering from fear and phobia.

Benefits of overcoming the fear
The benefits of dealing with and overcoming phobia and fear is immense and those who have recovered and overcome their fears and phobias have likened it to being reborn again, the world takes on new meaning when fears are dispelled. A new positive outlook develops which leads to living a happier and more fulfilled life, you start to feel good about yourself and what you can accomplish in life, you are finally free to do anything and everything that your heart desires.

While there might still occasionally be some anxiety for a time when confronted by your fear or phobia, it will be unlike the intense fear that once had you incapacitated from it. Once you have realized that the key to overcoming these feelings is inside you, the fear you feel doesn't have the same hold on you it once did and will eventually give up its hold on you altogether.

Overcoming dissociation

Dissociation causes us problems with our emotions, physical sensations and how we feel about ourselves as well as the world around us. It is often associated with depression and anxiety or when a person has gone through a traumatic experience. People suffering from dissociation offer have feelings of unreality and often fear they are going insane or that they have some incurable illness. Talking with and being around others becomes almost impossible and deep anxiety that is caused by the feelings can develop into a social phobia.

www.efhale.com   *   405-820-5845   *   efhale@efhale.com

The feeling of dissociation can vary from person to person depending on the circumstances that brought it about, but common thoughts and feelings associated with disassociation include:

- The world around feels unreal
- Not belonging in the world
- A grey fog covering their vision
- Like having a veil over your head
- The world is moving at a faster pace than normal
- Confusion
- A terrible feeling of not being able to cope
- Unsure of yourself
- Others find happiness but not you
- Extreme anxiety
- Feelings that everyone is against you
- Feelings that everyone is talking about you

These are just some of the feelings caused by disassociation and these feelings eventually cause the sufferer to believe that they have to turn deeper inward to themselves in order to get back into reality. They continually watch themselves for any brief glimpse that reality as they knew it is returning, of course the more they turn inward and worry the worse the symptoms are.

Cognitive behavioral therapy can help those suffering to overcome feelings of dissociation particularly when the cause is severe trauma. Those suffering from dissociation due to anxiety and stress may be able to rid themselves of the feelings through self-help methods and the help and understanding of a doctor.

It is important to remember that the world hasn't actually changed, it is only your perception of the world and those around you that has really changed and these are only temporary thoughts and feelings you are having. Once you have conquered and overcome what is causing the feelings of dissociation you will see things as you once used to. For those who suffer from feelings of dissociation due to depression and anxiety they should realize that the feelings are just that, no more than feelings and these feelings will leave in time. It is important not to be constantly studying them and wondering when they will go, try to accept that they are here for a time and give them no more thought. Once you have lost some interest in your feelings and are not constantly worrying about them it can be surprising how quickly the world once again becomes the world you once knew. Accepting your feelings and any thoughts you might have during this period is essential, for it is only when you lose fear of the situation can you recover.

Overcoming Doubt

Overcoming doubt is easy, if you don't doubt it, of course. However, most of us entertain an element of doubt in our minds about being successful whenever we try something new. In fact, almost everyone is in some way plagued with doubt of some kind. Take science, for example. Do you think all the scientific advancement achieved would have been possible without questioning the prevailing assumptions at the beginning? Suppose you want to start a business or launch a novel project. Are you absolutely sure that it will succeed? There is always a little fear or doubt at the beginning.

Despite your doubt, you cannot let it keep you from your ultimate goal. The reason is simple. You must be prepared to risk failure because it is important for overcoming doubt. Dive right in to whatever it is without being making rash decisions. Don't worry, you won't dive in without the right gear. You will analyze all of the possible consequences of your situation and you will embrace the outcome, whatever it may be. This is the secret to conquering doubt. Have courage to fight it out and you are sure to defeat it.

Belief is the enemy of doubt. Learn to think positively and believe in your ability to be successful. Remember you will succeed if you think you will and you will fail if you think that too. Your thoughts are self-fulfilling prophecies so you must stop thinking negatively. Likewise, never pay heed to the people who discourage you, who revel in planting doubts in you and who are actually wolves in sheep's clothing. Always be in the company of those people whose thoughts and attitudes to life in general are positive.

When failure strikes
You probably won't be fortunate to never experience failure in your life. However, you must understand that it is part of life. These are the times when failure fills your mind with doubt and it is hard to muster the confidence you built up earlier in the process. You can't let go of your commitment, no matter how shaken you are by failure. In fact, any setback should only prompt you to double your resolve to make another attempt at reaching your goal. In order for this to happen, train your mind to build your self-control and self-confidence. Every step towards self confidence helps get rid of doubt and you will be back to your successful ways once again.

Healthy doubt
Remember some amount of doubt can always be helpful in gaining wisdom or achieving advancement in life. But when it becomes a cause for your depression and inactivity or when it stands like an insurmountable hurdle in your way to reach your destination, draw upon your energy reserves that can toughen up your mind. You have to strengthen your will to succeed at all costs and weaken doubt by all possible means, so that you will lead a life of fulfillment.

You may succeed because of your doubt or in spite of your doubt. Or, you may have to accept the inevitable and compromise with whatever worst-case scenario that presents

www.efhale.com * 405-820-5845 * efhale@efhale.com

itself. If this happens, just change course, re-energize your cylinders and start afresh on your revised path. Defeat doubt before it defeats you.

Overcoming Feelings of Helplessness

We all come across feelings of helplessness to some degree or another sometime during our life, this is fine as long as we get back on track and overcome these feelings. However for some, feelings of helplessness set in and begin to affect our way of thinking and life. Here are some helpful tips to help you understand those feelings of helplessness and how to overcome them.

- Begin by identifying the problems, fears, issues and obstacles which make you feel helpless and try to discover why they make you feel this way
- Work on ways that encourage you to take on new beliefs that you can be independent, self-confident and are capable of dealing with anything that crops up in the future
- Learn ways to deal with these feelings of helplessness when they crop up
- Practice ways to deal with conflicts and problem solving when they arise
- If you have relapse and begin to doubt again remember that this is only normal and pick back up from where you left off
- Whatever the success however small be sure to reward yourself
- Realize that it will take time to change our feelings of helplessness so always strive towards your goals.
- Don't aim for perfection all the time, no one is perfect we all make mistakes
- Identify what you need to do to grow in the skills of self-coping, self-healing and self-confidence

Feelings of helplessness can cause us many problems in life, the longer you feel helpless, the less control you have over your own life; here are some common experiences that occur through helplessness.

- You begin to feel that no matter what you do or how hard you try you cannot succeed in life
- You become over dependant on others around you to help you overcome your problems
- You see yourself as totally incompetent
- You develop a deep seated fear that you are unable to handle a situation
- You become miserable, unhappy in life and depression sets in
- You think of yourself as a victim that always needs rescuing from situations
- You have a pessimistic outlook on life in general
- Your are afraid others see you as being frail and weak
- You become despondent because you run out of people who are willing to look after you by solving your problems
- You resign yourself to the fact that you will always be helpless, that you cannot possibly change

There are many ways you can help yourself overcome these feelings, the important thing to remember is that you are not alone and you can take back control over your life and make important decisions again to successfully solve your problems. All you need is to have faith in yourself and dig deep and find that faith and bring it to the surface. While we all have the ability to overcome our problems ourselves, it doesn't hurt to get advice from friends and relatives as long as you aren't relying on them totally to solve your problems for you.

www.efhale.com * 405-820-5845 * efhale@efhale.com

Overcoming Inner Conflicts

Commitment makes life a lot easier to deal with, by making a decision and sticking to it no matter what and staying committed without letting unwanted thoughts drift into your mind you are able to deal with any obstacle in your way. Inner conflicts lead us nowhere but to indecisiveness and are an open invitation to stress and losing confidence in ourselves.

While we all have them at sometime or another it is important that we know how to deal with them and resolve them and move forward with a positive attitude again, by resolving inner conflicts you are able to vastly improve your self-esteem, allow yourself to be more focused, and feel less stressed, listen to your inner voice and guide yourself when it comes to making choices and decisions, be in total control over your life, manage and achieve goals that you have set out in life, and create a healthier more relaxing and happier future.

Inner conflicts play havoc with our emotions and they lead to low self-esteem, low self-confidence and depression. With this in mind, it is essential to banish inner conflicts when they arise and don't let them start taking over. Inner conflict can develop in different ways it may stem from indecisiveness or deep-seated feelings stemming from unresolved issues in your life, they could even stem back from things that happened in your childhood. After all the person you are now is the result of what has happened throughout your life, instead of dealing with the unresolved issues you perhaps built up a wall and kept them in rather than facing them and dealing with them. It is essential that you break down the wall and bring these out into the open and deal with them now, overcoming unresolved issues and inner conflicts relies on:

- Letting go of the past and beliefs from the past including letting go of old habits and emotions, discovering the true inner you and listening to the inner you

www.efhale.com * 405-820-5845 * efhale@efhale.com

- Realize that you are capable of helping yourself and becoming the person you truly are
- Learning to become focused and centered on yourself, realizing what stresses you and why
- Making yourself let go of the feelings and thoughts you harbor relating from past issues
- Visualizing the new you, the more confident and decisive you until it becomes a reality

There are many courses, self-help books, DVDS and audio CDS which can help you to overcome past unresolved issues and so overcome and deal with inner conflicts. However there is no magical cure and it will take time to resolve these issues and start seeing a better way of dealing with and coping with life. While some of us change merely by using self-help methods others get more benefit from attending meeting groups of seeing a therapist in the early stages. It is important to realize however that you can change and only you can do it, whichever method you choose to take to get you there. It all basically comes down to the same thing, changing your feelings and thoughts.

Overcoming Intimidation

Intimidation can happen everywhere, in all walks of life and can occur in any age group. Being intimidated by someone is a form of being bullied, it happens in school, the workplace by co-workers or the boss, when shopping and in many other situations.

Some people are not even aware that they are being intimidated, while for it others it can make their life a misery day in and day out with them suffering intimidation on a regular basis. You might even be the one who is intimidating others.

www.efhale.com * 405-820-5845 * efhale@efhale.com

People who are constantly intimidated go through many feelings, but there are many steps that you can take to help eliminate intimidation. In order to be able to deal successfully with intimidation you first have to understand what intimidation really is, it can come in many disguises.

- Using force to get what you want from others
- Threatening to or using power and control to get others to do what you want
- Getting others to believe they are more powerful than you
- Using size or strength to get others to do what you want or threaten them
- Holding punishments over their head such as being fired, spanking or divorce
- Being quick tempered, angry or getting into a rage with someone to get them to do what you want
- Behaving in a manner that has others frightened to step up to you
- Using your wealth to get others to do what you want
- Using racial or sexual slurs towards others

There are many steps you can take to stop allowing others to intimidate you, the first step you should take is to look at yourself and determine if your irrational, unhealthy way of thinking has allowed yourself to become intimidated by others. If you think this might have been the case then you should take steps towards

- Identify new healthier ways of thinking to help you overcome and respond to the intimidating factors
- Display your new ways of thinking and acting to those who are intimidating you, this will show them that you are no longer willing to be intimidated by them
- Develop ways of dealing with people in case they respond negatively to the new you
- See the consequences of your new assertive behavior

www.efhale.com * 405-820-5845 * efhale@efhale.com

- Stick to your guns and accept whatever the consequences are of your new behavior

The next step to take once you have developed a strategy for dealing with those who intimidate you is to develop ways to reinforce your beliefs in the new you. The easiest way is to use daily affirmations or positive self-talk. Examples of positive self-talk include.

- I am a good person, who is worthy and deserves to be treat with respect
- I will not put anyone in a superhuman position over me
- I will take my life back under my control from any who tries to intimidate me in the future
- I will not allow others to intimidate me
- There is no one out there who can intimidate me

Overcoming the need to be in control

Some of us have problems when it comes to being in control, we simply have the urge to control all aspects of life for those around us and this can lead to many problems. There are many negative effects that come with the compulsive need to fix everyone's problems and they can have a severe effect on your life in general. So what is the need to be in control or to fix? In addition, what are the negative effects? And how can you help yourself to give up the need to be in control?

You could be said to have issues of needing to be in control if any of the following apply to you or someone you know.

- You compulsively go to someone's rescue, regardless of whether they ask for your help or not, just because you believe it is the way the task or situation should be dealt with.
- The feeling that other people are in need becomes an automatic response to you.

- You strongly believe that things have to be perfect or just right for people; otherwise, they cannot possibly be happy in life.
- You feel you have to change people because you cannot accept them as they are
- You strongly believe that you know what is best for others and try your best to make them see things your way.
- You accept personal responsibility for the actions of others.
- You cannot help but give advice to others or offer your help to them.
- People see you as interfering in their lives.
- You have a strong need to feel wanted or needed which leads to you becoming overly involved in the business of others.
- Things don't feel right if you are not helping others or fixing their problems.
- The most common negative effects that compulsive behaviour such as this can have on a person includes
- You develop relationships where people become overly dependant on you
- You cannot remain emotionally uninvolved if you come across someone you see as needing your help.
- You lose friendships due to you needing to be in control over their lives.
- You begin to neglect your own needs in favour of dealing with others around you.
- You are ridden with guilt if things don't improve for a person.
- You might become angry with those you have helped if they don't show enough recognition for what you have done.
- You develop low self-esteem through losing yourself with others.

- Ways which you can develop to overcome the need to be in control are

www.efhale.com * 405-820-5845 * efhale@efhale.com

- Have the belief that others have the ability to fix their own problems.
- Set up a boundary between those you think need your help.
- Don't get hooked on needing recognition from others.
- Accept that the only person you should control is yourself.
- Tell people to confront you if you try to give them unwanted help or advice.
- Realize that people have the ability to change themselves if they should want to.
- Only offer help to those who clearly ask for it.

Overcoming Trauma

There are many thoughts and feelings associated with a traumatic experience, trauma occurs when we are faced with any terrible situation, such as a car accident, fire, witness to an accident, natural disaster, an attack on your person, war, e.t.c. Many people who are recovering from a traumatic experience mentally block out the experience that caused distress while others will relive it time and time again. Trauma can bring many feelings such as

- Shock – shock is a normal reaction to any traumatic experience and the closer you were to the experience the more shock sets in. Your brain has to process the terrible images you have seen and this is when the feelings of shock set in and will take time to digest.
- Disbelief – many people experiencing a shocking situation have strong belief that what they have witnessed cannot possibly have happened.
- Denial – many people deny that the event happened; they try to force it out of their mind.

www.efhale.com * 405-820-5845 * efhale@efhale.com

- Emotional pain – even if you haven't been hurt in the incident you will feel the pain of those around you who did.
- Anger – after shock, anger will set in, you will ask yourself "why has this happened to you" and you can feel anger towards anyone and everyone.
- Blame – we very often blame ourselves or others for what has happened, we may even blame God for letting this happen.
- Sadness – when overcoming a particular traumatic experience you will feel waves of sadness suddenly overwhelming you.
- Depression – for some time after the experience you may suddenly lapse into depression from time to time.
- Anxiety – anxiety often develops from fear and can continue for some time after the experience.

All of the above are the most common feelings and thoughts associated with having gone through trauma; these feelings can come in no particular order and at any time. What you should realize is that these feelings are only natural and are your body and minds way of coping with what happened, the feelings and thoughts will eventually dissipate with time. There are many ways you can cope with them and help yourself to overcome them, the best way for you of course will depend on the severity of the trauma you were exposed to. There are however a number of coping skills which can be learnt in order to help you overcome trauma.

- Taking about what happened and letting it all out
- Listening to and accepting advice from family, friends or counselor
- Accepting what happened and continuing on with life
- Changing your environment
- Taking part in recreational activities
- Picking up your old daily routine
- Taking part in seminars

www.efhale.com * 405-820-5845 * efhale@efhale.com

Chapter IV: Becoming an Optimistic Individual and Achieve Goals in Life

Developing your self-image

How you see yourself goes a long way to how you feel about yourself and how others see you and think of you. If you think positively on the inside then you will glow with confidence on the outside and come across this way to others. Feeling good about yourself is essential if you are to be happy in life and make the most out of life, it can make the difference of you being successful or failing, it is all about how you see your self-image.

People suffer from low self-esteem for many reasons and if they have been brought up feeling negatively about themselves then developing a positive self-image will be difficult, but not impossible. Developing a positive outlook is about changing your thoughts and feelings about yourself and if you have been thinking negative thoughts for a long time changing the habit will take time. However by adapting a new way of thinking and sticking to this new way of thinking you will eventually banish unwanted negative feelings and will automatically replace them with positive ones in your day to day life. When this happens your outlook changes and with your outlook, you change, where once you might have thought something would be beyond your capabilities you will now look at it in a different light and begin to realize it is within your grasp.

There are many ways which you can use to develop a more positive self-image and esteem, there are self-help books dedicated to the subject, audio sessions which you listen and follow, DVDS, hypnotherapy audio or attending counseling sessions. They all however rely basically on the same principle, understanding what confidence really is, gaining confidence in yourself, ridding yourself of negative beliefs and replacing them with positive ones and learning strategies which allow you to remain confident in any situation.

The basics behind developing a more positive outlook and self-image are

- Thinking about positive self-image and confidence and understanding what it means to you
- Getting to know yourself better, recognizing your strengths and building on those strengths
- Moving forward and constantly changing negative thoughts into more positive ones
- Reflecting on what you have learnt and seeing the positive changes you are making to your life

We all talk to ourselves at one time or another, and we may find ourselves continually putting ourselves down and are very slow to praise ourselves. This must be changed. We want to change unhelpful self-talk and replace it with positive and encouraging self-talk, the easiest way to do this is by

- Getting rid of irrational thoughts and replace them with rational ones
- Replace negative thoughts and feelings with positive
- Give yourself credit
- Repeat positive affirmations to yourself when needed throughout the day

Change the Shape of Your Self-Image

While we all understand the importance of eating healthy, exercising and dieting, very few realize that changing our self-image is just as important to leading a healthy lifestyle. How you think and feel about yourself goes a long way to bringing happiness and success into your life and in order to change

www.efhale.com * 405-820-5845 * efhale@efhale.com

your self-image - just as you give your body a workout - you need to give your mind a work-out too.

The first step you need to take is to determine what exactly it is you would like to be and what you are already good at or enjoy doing. You might say you are good at sports, poetry and spending time with friends. The one thing you don't want to do is create a list of things that you don't like about yourself. This would only make you feel inadequate and hinder your ability to change yourself and your self-image. By focusing on the good in yourself, you will be able to quickly change your self-image into something that you are proud of.

Visualization and affirmations can help you to realize just how great you already are. See yourself doing and becoming everything that you originally wrote down. Repeat positive affirmations throughout the day to help the new way of thinking sink in and develop your new positive outlook. By vividly imagining this new you, your mind will retrain until you understand that all the things you visualize are true.

Consider keeping a jouranal
During this process you will benefit from keeping a journal about your transformation, you will be able to look back on it and this will help to strengthen your self-image and reinforce the new you. It is important that you let your past go and think only about the future and the new you, you will develop your new self-image more rapidly by focusing on what you are achieving and have yet to achieve.

Goals will get you there
You can help yourself mold a positive self-image if you set attainable goals for yourself and then strive to reach them. Giving yourself something to work towards creates success in your life – a vital part of reshaping your self-image. Set goals for yourself in any area you wish, work, personal, health, fitness and then go for it. Set yourself a realistic time in which to accomplish each goal and give yourself praise when you get there.

www.efhale.com * 405-820-5845 * efhale@efhale.com

How you choose to change your self-image is entirely up to you, there are no limitations to what you are able to achieve if you set your mind to it and are determined to work towards reaching the desired goal. If you stray from the path leading you there, then don't be put off and discouraged, get back on track and carry on with determination.

You are committing yourself to working hard to achieve what you want. Plan on what you will do when you finally reach your ultimate goal, you should aim to give yourself a special treat, you deserve it. Make sure that it is something which you can set your mind on during the tough times, keeping it in mind will give you an incentive that it will completely worthwhile.

How keeping a journal can help you succeed

You should never underestimate the power of keeping a written journal, there are many ways in which a journal can help you to better succeed in life. You can use it to help yourself associate your feelings with your thoughts and your thoughts with your feelings and this is what is most important in order to succeed in life. Your journal can help you to find out what motivates you in life, develop new skills, learn new strategies for dealing with life in general, write down ideas and plan them through and find out more about the person you are by asking questions of yourself and writing down answers to those questions. A journal is an essential tool when it comes to learning about ourselves and if we want to be a success in life, and knowing about ourselves is a must. While we may think, we know ourselves very few of us actually do. By keeping a journal, we begin to realize all the little things we do not truly know or understand about ourselves.

www.efhale.com * 405-820-5845 * efhale@efhale.com

Develop your intuition

Your own intuition is your greatest asset and if more people developed an ear to listening to what we are actually saying inside then more of us would know the way to go and how to successfully achieve what it is we want out of life, simply by following our own inner guidance. Your own personal journal can be a great way of developing your intuition and listening to yourself and what lies within you, record all the little things that you might let pass you by, such as flashes of inspiration, premonitions or hunches about something, basically anything that your intuition is telling you.

Keeping a journal is essential because inspiration can strike at anytime, some of the greatest inventors and thinkers kept journals including one of the most prolific inventors in history, Thomas Edison. One of the most helpful things a journal does is give us the ability to look back on records and refer to them, for example if you encountered a problem and overcame it in the past and a similar problem crops up then you can reflect back and apply the same solution or adapt it for a more positive outcome. Your journal can remind you of past achievements and this goes a long way to building self-confidence and helping you succeed in life when things get tough and can help comfort you.

Learn from the past

A technique which is very popular and one which keeping a journal can help you accomplish is the "best-better" technique, this technique can be applied to any situation that crops up in life and simply relies on you looking back on the situation and finding what you liked about it or what you experienced from it and then deciding how you could do better next time or how you could have better experienced from it. The key to recovering from past mistakes and succeeding in the future is to learn from your mistakes but remember to focus on your strong points rather than your weak ones. If you concentrate more on your weak points rather than your strong ones then very often this leads to you unconsciously reinforcing them which then lead to low self-esteem and of course having a low self-esteem isn't positive. It is only by building on your strengths can you increase your self-esteem and your self-esteem is the crucial factor to understanding your weaknesses and correcting them and therefore building a positive outlook on life which greatly increases your chances of success. So by noting down your experiences in your journal you are able to look back on them and gain a clearer understanding of yourself and how you feel which ultimately determines how you think and how you think determines how successful you are in life.

Start Early To Combat Low Self Esteem

Healthcare providers know that there are many reasons why people suffer from low self esteem from chemical imbalance to lack of faith, opportunities, discipline and more. Many agree, though, that the number one cause of low self esteem is due to lack of positive feedback and love given to children during their early years.

What happens all too often is that children are born before their parents have matured enough to focus more clearly on their own adulthood, family and family values, in the race to succeed with a mate while both are working long hours, still trying to learn good work and life ethics and morals while being out from under parental influence, plus learning about family life together and extended family members during those early years. It's a lot all at once.

And often before the maturing adults realize they may be following in their own parent's footsteps, they repeat similar mistakes done to them in their own childhoods. For example, many parents simply do not let their children try and try again and make their own mistakes. And many parents do not offer sincere praise and compliments to their children, instead taking them and their efforts for granted in all too often a difficult, tough world today full of challenges.

Another important factor is that children most often truly believe in their hearts that all adults are right, and set their own values and feedback systems by them. However, unfortunately too many of these adults raising young children are still battling illegal substance abuse, gambling, alcohol abuse and other very important issues. The results are that these adults are simply not doing what's best for either themselves or their families, especially with their young children trying to follow along in their footsteps. What a drug or alcohol abuser does not see, for instance, is the harmful physical, emotional and often other abuse passed along to the children as the adults get and stay too caught up in their own self-focus.

In short, children and adults of all ages do need positive feedback and people to demonstrate in a sincere manner their care and concern. Start up young and encourage your mate and children to make good, healthy, positive choices. And when they fail at something, offer them hope and encouragement to try and try again.

Also encourage education, regardless of the level you have. Too many adults often 'say' they want their children to success, yet negate comments all through childhood in areas of advancing education. So do offer plenty of reading materials around the home, show by example and read yourself, encourage workshops, online classes, ebooks and more. Try to point out and help guide children and mates in their areas of their strengths like subjects in school (chess, math, music…), hobbies (crafts, musical instruments, singing…) and service to others (volunteer work, part time job).

www.efhale.com * 405-820-5845 * efhale@efhale.com

Reach out and show positive feedback. And reach out with human love, care and respect. You'll gain in return, increasing your own self esteem and love.

Stop underestimating your worth

It is important that you do not under estimate your worth, as you are what you think you are, self-esteem is all about thoughts and what you think of yourself. If you think confidence then you will appear confident, and then this will show on the outside, when people realize their worth, they are able to face life with greater confidence and optimism about the future. They are more likely to be able to reach their goals and gain experience, satisfaction and happiness from life, are better able to form lasting relationships that work and are better able to cope with whatever life throws at them. A person who realizes their self-worth is a happy well adjusted person who posses the ability to cope with anything and anyone throughout their life and is capable of doing anything they set their mind on doing.

Problems caused by under estimating your self-worth
Many problems can occur in your life simply by under estimating your own self-worth, a lack of self-worth affects your sense of well being, causes problems with your feelings and needs, affects your ability to make good healthy choices in relationships, work and life in general and cause fears such as abandonment and problems such as people continually striving for perfection but never seeming to reach it. A lack of self worth has been attributed to being indecisive, addictions such as smoking, drinking, drug abuse, compulsive shopping disorder and problems with eating such as bulimia and anorexia.

Realizing your self-worth

www.efhale.com   *   405-820-5845   *   efhale@efhale.com

Each one of us is capable of realizing our self-worth, we do not have to do anything special in order to gain or deserve self-esteem. The key to realizing your self-worth is getting that little voice inside your head to stop putting you down all the time, it is our own thoughts and feelings that drive us to develop a low self-esteem. This little voice has developed over a long period of time, casting self-doubt onto ourselves until we genuinely believe that we aren't worthy or capable, it is our own minds that develop our feelings of low self-esteem, not some outside force. There are several ways in which you can begin to change your pattern of thought and boost your self-esteem that in turn begins the process of realizing your true self-worth, the basics behind making this correction are:

- Learning to recognize self-critical thoughts and stopping them
- Learning to replace self-thoughts with more positive ones
- Sticking with the habit of correcting your negative thoughts with more positive ones

There are many ways in which you can begin to set the pattern of changed thoughts but perhaps the easiest one is using affirmations, which are simple positive statements and using these to replace any negative thoughts, examples of positive affirmations could be:

- This is a new and exciting challenge – this could be used to replace thoughts such as this is too hard or I can't do this it's beyond me.
- I am a confident, worthy individual – replace this when you have thoughts such as can I do this or I could never do this.
- I can do anything my heat desires if I put my mind to it – this can be used to replace thoughts such as I'm not sure if I'm capable of completing this task or I don't know if I can complete what is asked of me.

All of these are simple affirmations that you can use to gradually change the way you think, which in time will change

www.efhale.com * 405-820-5845 * efhale@efhale.com

the way you feel about yourself and encourage you to realize your true self-worth.

www.efhale.com * 405-820-5845 * efhale@efhale.com

Developing your full potential

While many of us are happy in life and do accomplish to some extent what we set out to do, there aren't many that actually push themselves that little bit further and go on to develop their full potential. While we might be particularly good at doing certain things in life we could excel if only we had the courage and belief in ourselves to go for it.

As children we are full of excellent ideas, they never stop flowing because we have an open mind and belief in ourselves that we can accomplish just about anything. However, as we grow up fear of if we are doing the right thing and of speaking out and being ridiculed takes over and we stem the flow of our imagination and ideas. We hold back our thoughts and this can stop us from developing our full potential.

There are many ways you can start developing your potential, it's never too late. You should remember that there is no right and wrong way of thinking and many times the reason why others try to make you feel inferior when you voice opinions and ideas is because they wish they had had the idea and courage to speak up. So focus on your skills and abilities and let your thoughts run free, put them to use and truly excel in life.

In order to be successful you should realize that you will sometimes make mistakes, no one is perfect and mistakes are ok providing you acknowledge them and learn from them. Characteristics that you can nurture and that will lead to developing your true and full potential include:

- Working hard – putting your all into everything you do when working towards what you want in life
- Having patience – things don't happen overnight so have patience and you will be rewarded

www.efhale.com   *   405-820-5845   *   efhale@efhale.com

- Determination – stick to your guns and never give in when things don't go your way or you come across hurdles
- Commitment – be committed towards your goals and what you what to achieve, set goals in mind and don't let anything or anyone stand in your way of reaching them
- Organizational skills – the more organized you are the easier the road to success will be, plan out your ideas to their fullest before putting them into action
- Learn from mistakes – you will make mistakes along the way but you can learn valuable lessons from these and move on
- Confidence in yourself – you have to be self-confident and believe in yourself and your ideas, there is no room for doubt
- Stay realistic – don't set yourself goals that you cannot realistically achieve in a set amount of time, by setting yourself unrealistic goals you are setting yourself up for failure again and again.

When developing your full potential the two most important things to remember are, what you want out of life and what you can realistically do to make that possible. Once you have these facts clear then you can go full steam ahead towards achieving what you want.

Boost your Self-Esteem by Running

Running is a great self-esteem booster, especially if you are a beginning runner. Running will allow you to test and expand your limits like never before. With each milestone you reach you will find yourself more confident and able to take on the world.

Starting out slow reaps big rewards

www.efhale.com   *   405-820-5845   *   efhale@efhale.com

Even if you can't run to the mailbox without huffing and puffing, you can run to boost self-esteem. The first time you run to the mailbox, down the street, around the block or whatever distance it is, you will feel a great sense of pride and accomplishment. The first time you go out, you will probably do a lot more walking than you will running. However, if you keep at it, you will soon find yourself running more and more until one day your run the entire route without stopping.

The important thing to remember is to start out slow and not overdo it in the beginning. Your body does need to adjust to your new activity levels, especially if you previously lead a sedentary lifestyle. Overdoing it and causing overuse injuries can be a big discouragement, especially after seeing the progress that you made. Most people won't want to increase their weekly mileage by more than 10%. However, do what works best for you, some people can handle a larger mileage increase and others need to increase the mileage much more slowly.

Running is 90% mental
Despite how your muscles may feel, 90% of running is purely the mental capacity to be able to do it. Building up this side of your brain by telling yourself you can do it, you can finish the race, you can run for 30 minutes non-stop, or whatever your goal is will invariably be a surefire way to build up your self-esteem. What happens is that while running, in order to finish, you will have to come up with some good things to say to yourself, often referred to as positive self talk. This self talk not only gets you through your current run, but will start seeping into the rest of your life and you'll find yourself using it at work, while doing dishes and burdensome tasks will no longer feel so bad.

Goal setting
With running, you can set goals large and small. For the beginning runner, a good goal might be to complete a local 5k. You with undoubtedly enjoy the sense of accomplishment – not to mention the bragging rights at the office.

www.efhale.com * 405-820-5845 * efhale@efhale.com

Remember to set realistic goals for running and you'll build up your self-esteem – and miles – much faster.

How to Unearth Your Hidden Strengths

Have you ever realized that you, like anyone else, have a gold mine of strengths deep down within yourself? Most of us are unaware of the fact that we possess such hidden talents. The rest of us, even if we know that they are there within us, do not know how to bring the strengths out into the open and put them to use in improving the quality of our life or in leading a more fulfilling life. Let us explore ways and means of unearthing our hidden strengths to enrich our lives.

To begin with, you must believe that you have some inherent strengths. Banish all negativity in thought and action. Never say to yourself, "I can't. I don't have it within me." Instead, think that you have the strength within you to encounter any situation, no matter what that is, and that you can, and you surely will, succeed in dealing with it in an appropriate manner. Remember, self-belief is confidence and gaining confidence is half the battle.

The next step is to start exploring your self. Closely examine your background, the genetic as well as the acquired. Not that you have not done this before. You might very well have. Now you need to do it more systematically. Write down what you inherited from your parents or grandparents. If you don't think you've inherited any, think about what they have taught you. Is it possible that somewhere deep within you, you have those very strengths, but you have not realized that you could use them? List all the strengths and talents of your parents or grandparents. See if some or all of them you can put to use. For instance, does music run in the family? Did you ever notice that your mother had tons of patience? You too may have it within you, without being aware of it. Have you ever noticed that you have, by nature, a way with words that others you know do not have? Have you not put this skill to good use? Maybe you are endowed with a strong physique, but you are not aware of the ways in which your physical strength can be utilized profitably. Explore, experiment and, finally, exploit. That should be your strategy in drawing out your strengths into the open.

Educational strengths
Your acquired background appears to you to be easier to analyze. But actually it needs a more detailed examination. Again, draw up a detailed list of the strengths your education and training have given you. What is the skill set you have acquired? Are you utilizing your skills and your talents to their fullest extent? Have you pursued your interests, converted some of them into hobbies, and thought of the possibility of turning at least one of the latter into a second profession? Enlist your inner strengths like composure, compassion, conflict-resolution, self-control, perseverance or determination etc. for achieving success in your life.

This is not once in a lifetime exercise. As your life keeps progressing, periodical reviews of your strengths help you pinpoint unknown strengths that may help lead you down the right path. Who knows, you may strike gold!

How NLP Can Help You

Chances are that many of those who first come across NLP wonder what it is all about, even if it appears in the context of influencing human behavior through the adoption and practice of certain established techniques and procedures. Actually, NLP stands for Neuro-linguistic Programming, where 'neuro' is something related to both mind and body, 'linguistic' is about language patterns or structures and 'programming' is devising ways and means of coordinating mind, body and language for shaping behavior so as to achieve better results than before in various walks of life. In a sense, NLP can help you in many ways, if only you get to know its techniques and how to use them for your benefit.

Changed perceptions

You can turn to NLP when you are interested in developing your personality traits and characteristics, which determine your verbal and non-verbal reactions to the happenings in this world. As a first step, let us understand that your perception of reality is based on your subjectivity. Just as a map is merely a miniature representation of a territory, what you perceive as real is only a colored representation of reality, not the reality itself. You can't help but look at the world through rose-colored glasses. Your reactions are dictated not by the reality but by your view of that reality. NLP helps you in realizing this and reducing, if not completely removing, your subjectivity. You will then perhaps consider adopting alternative viewpoints of reality and, consequently, bringing about a shift in the way you react to it.

Why do people react differently to a particular event or situation? Is it not because of the differences in their individual perceptions of that event or situation? What a traumatic event is to one may not be the same to another. For instance, some people may take verbal or physical abuse lightly or simply ignore it. Others may be so affected by it that they need psychological or medical treatment. The underlying philosophy of NLP is based on the premise that it is possible to change one's perceptions, beliefs and behavior so that traumatic experiences become possible to treat. It is also possible that you might even become immune to trauma.

Get rid of phobias

You can similarly get rid of your phobias, if any, by going into the factors that cause your fear in the first place, with the help of NLP techniques. You can perhaps look at things in the way that your adversaries do. You can perhaps consider the same things from a totally new perspective. Or, you can perhaps study people who have achieved excellence in any particular aspect of their life, find out what qualities and factors contributed to their success and then try and import the same or similar factors and qualities into your life in an effort to achieve excellence in your chosen field. You can lower your levels of unhappiness or raise the levels of happiness by transforming your belief portfolio, your pre-conceived notions, your language patterns that display your innermost feelings, your unconscious mind that exposes your conscious reactions to the external world, and so on. In short, as the NLP practitioners claim, NLP transforms you into a new you, a happier you and a more effective you capable of dealing with this world in a much better way than before.

De-cluttering for success

If we are surrounded by clutter and disorganization in our lives it makes an excellent breeding ground for negativity, negativity is what brings about feelings of low self-worth and low self-esteem which hinders us in life and is the basis for us being unsuccessful in what we choose to do. It is essential therefore if we want to succeed and make the most out of life that we de-clutter from time to time and remove any excess obstacles and belongings from our path, keeping our lives open and free flowing. Here are some simple points to remember to keep your home and life clutter free.

Replace old with new
This applies to anything which you bring into your home be it clothing, utensils, furniture or any other item, if you continually buy and bring new items into your home then very quickly you are going to be over run with items which usually end up being packed in cartons and put in the basement. Even if you pack items and put them in the basement it is still clutter, clutter that you could do without so get into the habit of throwing things away or giving them to charity when you buy new.

Don't keep unnecessary things

www.efhale.com * 405-820-5845 * efhale@efhale.com

In order to keep your home clutter free it is essential that you don't keep anything which is not essential, items belonging in this category include junk mail which appears through your letterbox, flyers, old newspapers, magazines, letters or trash from your car. Letters that you don't need can be shredded immediately, the same for junk mail, while any trash from your car should be collected daily and disposed of immediately. It is surprising if you get into the habit how much junk you can eliminate building up in your home on a daily basis just by taking care with items such as this.

Throw anything away that you don't like
Never hang onto items simply because you were given them as presents, while this may sound harsh it leads to unnecessary clutter, if you don't like something then don't keep it, give it away to someone who likes it or sell it but don't hang onto it.

Have a goal
When looking around your home have a goal in mind when de-cluttering, for example treat each room separately and say to yourself "I aim to de-clutter this room by 25%". If you start out with a clear goal in mind you will feel more in control, organized and feel you are accomplishing something. You should divide the clutter into three piles, those items you can sell, the ones which are trash and those that you wish to give to charity, starting out with a clear plan and goal in mind makes de-cluttering your life so much easier.

Never procrastinate
Be harsh with yourself and don't feel guilty about throwing something away or giving it away, once you start de-cluttering don't give it a second thought and remove something from a pile and change your mind about getting rid out of sentiment. If we stop and think about every item in this way it sows the seeds of doubt and negativity that leads to disorganization and a home full of items we don't need.

www.efhale.com * 405-820-5845 * efhale@efhale.com

Get Private Coaching From Ethan Hale

You may rest assured that this book covered the topics to taking command of your life, your thoughts, and your self-esteem. If you would like to take yourself to even greater heights of personal ability and challenge feel free to contact me directly at the website, email address, or phone number listed in the footer, You may also contact me via skype at imefhale. Also, please make any suggestion or comments here: 3mmm@efhale.com. Finally, thanks for reading!

Made in the USA
Charleston, SC
06 September 2013